The World of Nature

BABY ANIMALS

GALLERY BOOKS
An Imprint of W. H. Smith Publishers Inc.
112 Madison Avenue
New York City 10016

This edition first published in U.S.
in 1990 by Gallery Books,
an imprint of W.H. Smith Publishers, Inc.
112 Madison Avenue, New York, New York 10016

ISBN 0-8317-9581-6

Printed and bound in Spain

For rights information about the photographs in
this book please contact:

The Image Bank
111 Fifth Avenue, New York, NY 10003

Producer: Solomon M. Skolnick
Author: Marcus Schneck
Design Concept: Lesley Ehlers
Designer: Ann-Louise Lipman
Editor: Joan E. Ratajack
Production: Valerie Zars
Photo Researcher: Edward Douglas
Assistant Photo Researcher: Robert V. Hale
Editorial Assistant: Carol Raguso

Title page: **When a new member of the
troop is born, all the monkeys and apes
in that group diligently accept parental
duties.** *Opposite:* **Kittens begin their
progression toward independence from
their mothers at about three weeks of age
with some prodding. The mother continues
to play with them, but becomes progressively
less tolerant of bothersome actions.**

Play behavior in kittens begins to decline at about five months, coinciding with the age at which the animals would begin to fend for themselves in the wild. *Below:* Each kitten in this litter is already well on its way to developing a distinct personality, a process that began when they were two or three weeks old.

E ven the most hard-bitten among us can't help letting loose a few "ooohs" and "aaahs" at the sight of a puppy bounding across the carpet after a toy, or a kitten pouncing on another's tail, or a clutch of fuzz-covered chicks pecking their way across the barnyard.

Baby animals hold a special place in the human psyche. Rush-hour traffic pulls to a standstill for a mother mallard and her trailing ducklings crossing the roadway. A gardener abandons a corner of his fenced-in vegetable patch to allow a cottontail rabbit to rear her nest of hairless babies in undisturbed safety. An avid deer hunter pauses to admire the spotted camouflage of a white-tailed fawn.

Every one of these tiny creatures represents life renewed, life continued. From the most familiar household pets and farm animals to the exotic creatures of far-off mountains and jungles, every living creature begins life as an infant version of the adult animal.

Top to bottom: **Puppies, such as these young beagles, have a universal appeal that seems to be shared by no other creatures. Patience is the key to photographing any young animals, which are generally boundless bundles of energy that rarely stay still. These curious hunting dog puppies survey their surroundings.**

Seemingly helpless, barnyard chicks are actually able to find their own food shortly after emerging from the eggs. *Below:* Chicks have been attracting human empathy for centuries, as chickens were among the first domesticated animals. The first written reference dates to 1400 BC China. *Opposite:* Chicks are among the first baby animals "discovered" by today's children, often in a "hatch-atorium" as part of an agricultural exhibit in the local shopping mall.

However, for most creatures on Earth, the baby does not look much like the adult. The caterpillar bears practically no resemblance to the butterfly; the tadpole can be identified as the infant frog only through previous knowledge. Many of these "lower" animals – the reptiles, amphibians, fishes, insects – emerge from their eggs independent of any parent and totally on their own. But the more advanced, more evolved animals – the mammals and the birds – generally start out dependent on their parents and, in some species, their extended families.

Even the most fearless predators start their lives as tiny, blind, helpless beings, totally dependent on their mothers. The mighty brown bear, for example, may grow to 1,700 pounds and fear nothing in its environment. But it begins as a hairless, one-pound creature, born while its mother hibernates.

Baby animals born or hatched in this totally dependent state, with their eyes closed and little or no hair or feathers, are described as altricial. Initially, they lack nervous and muscular coordination and can't survive on their own.

Ducklings, like chicks, imprint on the first moving thing that they see and then follow that thing wherever it leads. Normally this is their mother, but they've also been known to imprint on humans, dogs, and even objects.

Those animals that are born or hatched with their eyes open and their bodies covered with hair or feathers are referred to as prococial. They can scamper about and find their own food soon after they emerge. They can survive independent of the parent. Most animals produce this type of offspring, although the more evolved creatures tend toward altricial babies.

In brown bears, two is the average litter size. They will stay with their mother through two winters. Then, if she mates again, they will be driven off. The young males will leave their mother's territory entirely, while the young females will remain in the vicinity of their birthplace. If the mother does not mate at this time, she will spend a third winter denning with the cubs.

The male brown bear takes no part in raising his offspring. In fact, a great many of the 30 or 40 percent of the young bears that die before reaching maturity are killed by males.

The original "kids," young goats are constantly active and extremely difficult to restrain. *Below:* Common in many a barnyard, goats are generally born as twins, triplets, or quads.

For many rural residents, a snowy white lamb on a field of green is the embodiment of spring bursting out of winter. *Below:* The gentle, docile appearance of fleecy lambs belies the young animals' active nature and strong leaping ability. *Overleaf:* Piglets are born about 114 days after the sow has been bred. Two litters per year are possible in some breeds, if the farmer takes great care with the female.

Young pigs are extremely swift and possess quick reflexes, which is why greased pig contests remain popular attractions at county fairs across the country. *Below:* Baby pigs are called piglets, and shoats after they are weaned. As they grow, young females are known as gilts and later as sows. Mature males are boars or, if they cannot breed, barrows. *Opposite:* Calves are gangly but active, traits they gradually lose as they approach maturity.

The mother brown bear's instinct to protect her young is intensely strong and she will fight to the death to defend her cubs. This bond between the mother and her cubs is the strongest nature has to offer.

Such a strong link among the mammals is understandable. The female has carried the developing, new creature inside herself, sometimes for many

From awkward, knobby-kneed beginnings grow the stately, aristocratic thoroughbred horses of racing and show fame. *Left:* Small replicas of their parents, colts are able to run with their mothers within a few hours of birth. *Opposite:* Colts play by running, which is practice for the animal's principal means of survival in the wild.

months: in the case of the African elephant, about 640 days (more than 21 months); porpoise, 360 days (12 months); human, 267 days (about nine months); mountain lion, 93 days; dog, 65 days; hamster, 16 days; opossum, 13 days.

The female mammal then nurtures the baby through the important first days, weeks, and months of its life, providing it with milk produced by her own body. Only mammals have the specialized milk-producing glands known as mammaries, which are hormonally activated during the latter stages of pregnancy and which begin to produce milk when the baby is born. Exact content varies from species to species, but milk is generally composed of water, fats, minerals, proteins, and sugars. It provides all the nourishment that the infant mammal needs during the initial weeks or months of life, a period of incredible growth.

Top to bottom: **Baby gray squirrels are blind for the first 35–40 days of their lives and they won't be fully furred for another 14 to 21 days. Hoary marmots are born in midsummer and spend their first winter in hibernation with their parents. Very early in life, skunks are able to use their anal scent glands to spray a defensive liquid at potential aggressors.** *Opposite:* **Young rabbits, like this cottontail, are born blind, naked, and totally dependent upon their mothers. Hares, by contrast, are precocial babies, born with open eyes, a fur coat, and the ability to fend for themselves.**

The bonds created last for varying amounts of time. An African elephant will suckle from the mother for up to four years and female offspring may live their entire lives in the mother's herd. Conversely, less than 20 days after birth, young white-footed mice part from their mother.

Baby raccoons are among the most curious and investigative wild babies, and learn the skills the omnivorous creatures will need throughout their lives by playing. *Left:* Raccoons, young and old, spend a great deal of time in and near water, but they do not wash everything before eating.

Young gray foxes are tended by both parents, although their father has a nearby den separate from the rest of the family. *Below:* Litters of coyote puppies vary greatly in number, from as few as one to as many as 18. The reproductive capacity of the mother increases and decreases with changes in the animal's environment and population.

In many animal families, such as horses, cattle, deer, and antelopes, the mother is the only parent the baby ever knows. And even "mom" is of little help to any offspring that is unable to run with the herd within just a few hours of birth.

Female caribou, which annually migrate to calving grounds in the Arctic and then travel back below the treeline, continue along their inborn itinerary an amazingly short time after the baby is born. Any young one that falls behind will be abandoned after a bit of prodding from its mother and become a meal for bears or wolves.

Yet, these same animals will nurse their offspring longer than the seemingly more protective predator parents. Those young caribou that are able to keep up with the herd may still be suckling a year after birth.

Preceding page: Once an increasingly rare sight in much of the eastern United States, white-tailed fawns are now born in incredible numbers each spring. Scientific game management has made this species of deer the most widespread big game on the continent. *This page:* During the first year of its life, the white-tailed fawn takes nearly all of its cues from its mother—particularly her large white flag of a tail. *Right:* For the first several days of their lives, white-tailed fawns remain quite still, taking advantage of their spotted coat of camouflage and their odorless bodies to avoid predators.

In other species – many of the monkeys and apes, for example – the infant is given a shorter period before it is weaned from the mother's milk, but a relatively long period before it must fend for itself. The father is an active participant in the rearing of his offspring. The male titi monkey of South America, for example, assumes the primary caregiver role. He is the parent who carries the baby for about five months until it is weaned, and gives it up only for nursing by the mother and occasionally for carrying by the baby's older siblings.

Evolution has favored caring parents, because it is generally the genes of the best and most successful parent animals that are passed onto future generations.

But caring for the young sometimes extends beyond the mother and father of a baby animal. Many of the monkeys and apes engage in infant-directed activity across the entire band or troop.

In wild dog packs, such as the wolf, social hierarchy permits only the dominant male and female to breed and produce subsequent generations. This privileged position may be given voluntarily by the lesser members of the pack, or it may be enforced by the dominant animals.

Mother and calf elk communicate in a series of neighs from the former and bleats from the latter.

Less than an hour after birth, the bison calf gets to its feet to nurse from its mother. In another couple of hours the calf can walk about, and after two days is ready to accompany its mother and the herd. *Below:* Female moose are extremely protective of their calves, even to the point of taking on attacking brown bears. *Opposite:* Mountain goat kids are generally born on a mountain ledge, secluded from the rest of the herd that they will join within a few days. *Overleaf:* Young mountain goats' hooves are perfectly designed for life on the ledges. The outer rim is hard and sharp to provide a firm grip, while the softer sole provides traction.

Bighorn lambs are well-developed at birth, with open eyes, a soft wool coat, and tiny horn buds. *Below:* Lambs of the Dall sheep, which are walking just three hours after birth, begin to graze on grasses at only 10 days. *Opposite:* Black bear cubs are able climbers and this is their principal means of escape from danger. They retain this ability throughout adulthood.

As the black bear extends its range into areas with more human population, these little bundles of black are becoming regular sights. *Below:* Fishing is an important skill to the brown bear, one that the mother teaches to her cubs early on. *Opposite, top:* The average polar bear litter is two cubs, although up to four are not uncommon. *Bottom:* These polar bear cubs, which might grow as large as 1,200 pounds, began life at less than two pounds. They were born in their mother's winter den, under the snow.

But the non-breeders exhibit no resentment toward the offspring of this exclusive scheme, and regularly aid in the rearing, feeding, and protection of the babies. This may occur because the non-dominant animals realize that the entire pack will benefit from larger numbers for the hunt. Or, it may occur through a process known as kin selection, whereby the non-dominant wolves lend their assistance for the benefit of the young because those offspring share much of the same genetic base, nearly as much as would their own offspring.

In such highly social animals, interactions with the group are essential to transform the young animal into a normally functioning adult.

Birds come the closest of all other animals to the mammals in caring for their young. Although a few, like the brown-headed cowbirds (which drop their eggs off in the nests of other species for those birds to hatch and raise), are extremely poor examples of parenthood. Most put extreme amounts of energy into the care of the next generation.

Top to bottom: Young harbor seals are born in the springtime when the adult animals are gathered into small groups. Most seals and sea lions bear a single pup and it grows quickly on mother's milk which is composed of about 50 percent fat. Harp seal pups are born with a completely white coat and huge black eyes that constantly tear as a natural defense against the climate. *Opposite:* Emperor penguins carry their single egg and later, their chick, atop their webbed feet and next to their warm underbellies.

In most species both parents take an active role in building the nest, incubating the eggs, and feeding the nestlings until they fledge. The specific duties of each parent varies.

Both male and female black-capped chickadees, for example, excavate the nesting cavity in a rotting tree trunk and line it with feathers, animal hairs, moss, and other soft materials. The female then settles down to incubate the eggs, while the male maintains a near-constant schedule of flights to and from the nest, keeping his mate well-fed on insects. After the eggs have hatched and a half-dozen screaming, hungry babies fill the nest, both parents will hunt.

Nearly all birds construct some sort of cup-shaped nest for the laying and incubating of their eggs, from the cavity of the chickadees to the familiar mud-and-grass bowl of the American robin to the sanderling's grass-lined hollow. The cup shape is efficient in maintaining the high, even temperatures that are needed for incubating the eggs.

Preceding pages: **These large penguins live in colonies but do not share the feeding and rearing duties for one another's chicks.** *This page:* **Bald eagles build huge nests of sticks that they add to, and reuse, year after year.**

Although bald eagles were in severe decline for several decades, due to pesticide problems that caused them to lay thin-shelled eggs, their numbers are now on the upswing. *Below:* The national symbol of the United States begins life blind and helpless, with a coat of down that will eventually be replaced by feathers. *Opposite:* The bald eagle nestling may take up to 75 days before making its first flight. Later, when it has mastered this skill, it can reach flying speeds of more than 45 miles per hour.

Antarctica's emperor penguin
has evolved a completely different
means for incubating eggs in one
of the harshest environments on
the planet. The female lays her
lone egg and immediately leaves
on an extended fishing trip. The
male protects the egg from the
elements, including nighttime
temperatures as low as minus 80
degrees Fahrenheit. He immediately works the vulnerable egg
up onto his feet, next to his
warm underbelly, and holds it
there for the next two months.
He eats nothing during this
period, and merely waits for the
female to return when the chick
is almost ready to hatch. She
takes over for the male, who
finally rushes off to find some
fish of his own.

While mammals and birds
provide most of the animal
kingdom's shining examples
of parental care, devotion to the
next generation is not entirely
limited to these "higher" animals.
The female American alligator,
for example, remains close to her
mounded nest throughout the
nine weeks that it takes for the
sun to incubate her buried eggs.
When she hears the calls of her
hatchlings coming from the nest,
she digs them free. They will
remain with her for as long as
three years, often hitchhiking
rides on her long nose.

**Although rodents, such as the meadow
mouse, form the bulk of the food that
these parent red-tailed hawks will bring
to the nest for their chicks, the diet may
include everything from rabbits to snakes
and fish.**

The stickleback fish, various types of which appear in North America, Europe, and Asia, likewise provides early protection for its offspring, but through the male. During the 10 days the eggs incubate, the male swims close to the hollow ball of a nest that he built from vegetation, and guards his soon-to-hatch offspring from all comers. This protective behavior continues for a few days after the hatching, when the young fish leave the nest.

The social insects, such as ants, bees, and wasps, provide everything for the larvae and defend them against all threats in a way that seems similar to bird and animal parents' methods. In reality, these insects function more like a single animal than a collection of individual insects. Their concern for the next generation is an offshoot of the behavior that places the survival of the colony above the survival of the individual. Like so many animals, they

Top to bottom: **This herring gull chick won't acquire its full adult plumage until its third year molt. Herring gull chicks peck their way out of their eggs after about a month of incubation in their earth-based nest. Precocial chicks, herring gulls are able to move about and fend largely for themselves very shortly after emerging from the egg.** *Opposite:* **Baby egrets may be raised in nests ranging from on the ground to more than 30 feet up in the trees.**

have no concept of parent or family. Rather than careful, tender care of individual offspring, they rely on numbers to carry forth their kind. They definitely have no concept of play, which for most mammal babies is vital to the learning of skills needed for survival in later life.

Swan chicks hatch after about 35 days of incubation by their mother, with the father bird maintaining guard. *Below:* The male swan takes the first hatched cygnet from the nest to the water, while the female remains on the nest to incubate the rest of the eggs.

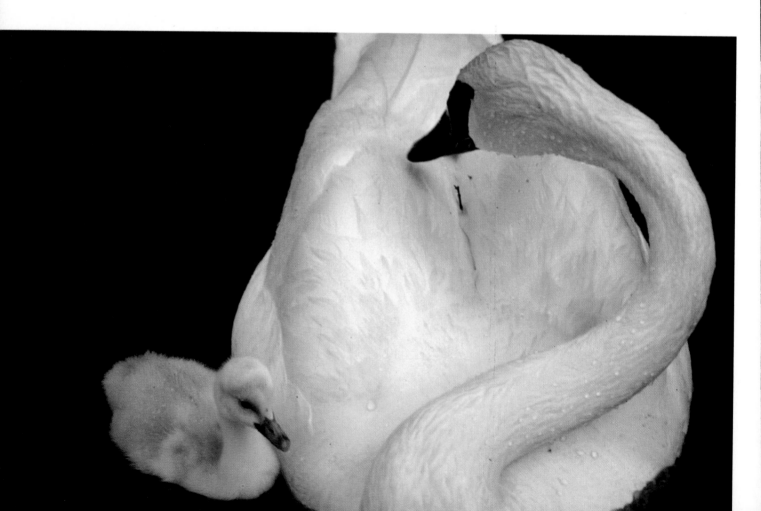

A black-winged stilt hovers near its young. *Below:* The baby frigatebird stays in the nest an incredible 150 to 200 days before taking its first flight.

With its chick on its back, the western grebe dives for fish. *Below:* The red-throated loon raises its chicks in isolation from other nests, usually in a large mound of mud and plant material.

To a predator like the lion, hunting skills are a key to survival. Although all cats are born with some hunting instinct, the full execution through to the kill must be learned. The lion cubs gather these skills gradually by stalking and pouncing upon one another and their mother and by following the female while she hunts. Eventually they spread their playful "attacks" to the other members of the pride: their father, their aunts and uncles, other cubs.

They are tolerated, at times even encouraged, in this play by the other members of the social group, which help to feed the cubs so long as game is plentiful. In times of poor hunting, however, the cubs may be pushed away from the kill by the adult lions, even by their mother. If the unfavorable conditions persist, they may starve.

Play in baby animals can also take the form of imitation of their mother and, in social animals, others in the group.

Top to bottom: Like most nestlings, these baby red-winged blackbirds cry out for attention from their parents almost constantly. Although this male yellow warbler is giving an insect meal to a chick of its own species, they can frequently be seen feeding the parasitic chicks of the cowbird, because the yellow warbler is a principal target of the cowbird's foster-parenting plan. The speckled baby of the American robin is one of the first young birds people encounter, due to the common and widespread nature of the species.

Mountain gorillas, like many apes and monkeys, learn almost every action through imitation of the adults in the troop during the seven years before they reach maturity.

Individual apes raised outside of such group situations often do not acquire the skills and knowledge necessary to function properly. Females that have not witnessed the rearing of babies will not provide proper care for their own offspring and may even harm them. All such individuals will avoid the normal group activities, such as communal grooming.

Hooved mammals, such as horses, cattle, deer, and antelopes, have their own form of play, which involves practicing skills that will be essential in life. As escape-oriented creatures, much of this play focuses on running.

Baby birds generally do not engage in play. Parent birds, however, do a certain amount of "teaching" about acquiring food, and gradually force the babies to take items on their own.

Preceding pages: Great horned owl chicks are among the first hatched each year. The adult birds begin nesting in late January or early February. *This page, left:* Young koalas hitch rides through the trees on the backs of their mothers. *Below:* The joey must crawl from the mother's birth canal into her brood pouch within the first 30 minutes of its life. In the brood pouch, where it will remain for several months, the still-developing baby kangaroo attaches itself to its mother's teat. *Opposite:* Triplet calves are extremely rare in giraffes. A single baby is generally born 15 months after breeding.

Lion cubs engage in much play during the first months of life, practicing the hunting and fighting skills they will need in adulthood.

The lioness is a caring and gentle parent when the supply of prey is good. In harder times, though, her cubs may starve. *Below:* Two to four lion cubs are the normal litter. They are helpless and completely dependent upon their mother during the first several weeks of life. *Overleaf:* Eventually the lion cubs are accepted into the pride where their play will, at times, involve nearly all of the adult lions.

The young rhinoceros will stay with its mother for two to three years. *Below:* Rhinos are born without the magnificent horn that has led these animals to the brink of extinction at the hands of poachers. *Opposite:* African elephants have perhaps the strongest mother-baby bond in all the animal kingdom. A young female may eventually become part of the same herd as its mother.

Some young birds, such as chicks and ducklings, undergo a process known as imprinting. At an early point in their lives, they will identify with whatever moving thing they see first. Normally this is their mother, but under abnormal and experimental conditions the imprinting has involved dogs, humans, and even objects that were artificially moved in front of the young birds. Once the imprinting has taken effect, the chicks or ducklings will follow the imprinted object wherever it goes.

Animals have evolved a mystifying array of responses to the constant struggle for survival. Nowhere is this more evident than in the many ways they ensure the continuation of their genes and their species in the next generation and in the amazing diversity with which new animal life enters this world.

Preceding pages: These young African elephants, fresh out of a dunk in a watering hole, could grow to weigh more than 13,000 pounds. However, poaching for the valuable ivory tusks they will eventually grow could end their lives long before they reach that size. *This page, top to bottom:* Like most apes and monkeys, baby mountain gorillas need the socialization of the troop to grow into fully functioning, normal adults. Although care of the babies falls to their mother and some other females in the troop, the entire band will fight in protection of every individual. During their first several weeks of life, baby baboons ride on their mothers' backs. *Opposite:* Young chimpanzees stay with their mothers for as long as three years, and maintain close physical contact.

Index of Photography

TIB indicates The Image Bank.

By the same author

A Dog's
Little Instruction Book

- Don't drink from a bowl with CAT on it
- Keep your tail down when it's windy
- Make friends with the local butcher
- Never be seen in tartan
- Don't eat slug pellets (or slugs)
- Chase frisbees but not boomerangs
- When you get old, learn some new tricks

A Teddy Bear's Little Instruction Book

- Never serve your porridge then go out for a walk
  - Don't wear your duffle coat in the house
- If you're made of mohair, ponder on the nature of a mo
  - Don't be part exchanged for a computer game
    - Be brave – sleep with the light off
- Don't become a projectile in domestic disputes
  - Follow fashion – don't be the bear behind

Make nuisance phone calls

Pull faces when having a family
photograph taken

Share your breakfast with the dog

Pull your socks off at every opportunity

Be unsociable towards Mummy's friends' children

Bang on the table

In a toyshop, never settle for least expensive

In a sweetshop, never settle for a small packet

In a clothes shop, never settle for something tasteful

Never open your mouth for the dentist

Don't let Daddy bury you on a beach – it is inevitable that he will deliberately upset you by pretending to leave

Put your potty on your head

Blame your baby sister for your own misdemeanours

Demand to wear reins in department stores – just to slow Mummy down

Don't play with toys with an obvious 'educational' value

Stamp your feet when you can't get your own way

Always ask 'Why?', even if you know the answer

Drop something when crossing the road

Fall down the stairs the day the stairgate is left open

Giggle when you poop

Giggle when someone else poops, especially if they think they got away with it

Don't come home from shopping without a toy or some sweets

If there's water about, fall in it

Pester for horrid toys you've seen advertised on television

Stare at people you don't know

Perform the 'choke' test by putting everything in your mouth

Pull a knot in your shoelaces that is impossible for anyone to untie

Ask the baker for a gingerbread *person*

Make sure you get both Mum *and* Dad up at night

Manage to pull the safety eyes off your teddy

- Persuade Daddy to stick a rubber suction cup on his forehead so it leaves a bruise

- Rearrange Nana's ornaments

- Learn which parent is the softest touch

Make disparaging comments about a friend's parents' car

Whine for a biscuit, then say you don't like any of the ones on offer

Smile and you'll get your own way

- Bring new meaning to the phrase 'accident prone'

- Teach the dog bad habits

- Learn bad habits from the dog

- Learn to project your vomit accurately

- Dribble profusely when teething

- Pull old ladies' hair on the bus or train

- Unravel toilet rolls

- Post the front door keys through the letterbox

- Be computer literate by the time you're three

- Fall asleep when someone's talking to you

- Cut your own hair

- Wipe muddy hands on your clothes

- Never let parents forget a promise

- Put both feet in the same trouser leg

- Sneeze at talcum powder

Talk in church

Always be the centre of attention

Say your shoes hurt even if they don't, just so you'll get a new pair

Try out your new teeth, but not on yourself

Undo your own seatbelt

Spot the moral at the end of a cartoon

Scribble on important documents

Leave half sucked lollipops on the sofa

Leave toy cars on the stairs

Announce when you're going to the toilet, and describe your accomplishments when you return

Remember, your mummy loves you, even if everyone else thinks you're smelly, noisy, ugly and difficult

Establish your own sleeping routine

Give your soft toys really imaginative names, like 'Dog', 'Rabbit' and 'Mouse'

Bruise yourself in time for the appointment with the health visitor

Shut your fingers in cupboard doors

Grab the spoon when being fed

Run out of the lift when the doors are closing

Train an older sibling to be your unpaid slave

Bite fruit in the greengrocer's
and put it back

Three ways to wipe your nose
without a tissue:
a) On your sleeve
b) On someone else's jumper
c) With your tongue

Fall asleep in the car just as you're arriving somewhere

Climb over the stairgate

Get your head stuck in your playpen

Go rigid when you don't want to sit in your pushchair

Make sure your early paintings are treated with respect

Blow bubbles in your drink

Lock yourself in the toilet

Lock someone else in the toilet

Ruin 'quality time'

Cultivate a dirty laugh

🍼 Lift your dress in public

🍼 Lift Mummy's dress in public

🍼 Practise emotional blackmail – try 'Nobody loves me' when you're being ignored